HILLSBORO PUBLIC LIBRARIES
Hillsboro, OR
Member of Washington County
COOPERATIVE LIBRARY SERVICES

# The Library of the PILGRIMS

# The First Thanksgiving

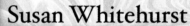

Susan Whitehurst

**HILLSBORO LIBRARY**
HILLSBORO, OR 97123

MEMBER OF WASHINGTON COUNTY
COOPERATIVE LIBRARY SERVICES

In eternal thankfulness to Rosemary, Don, and Angel

Published in 2002 by The Rosen Publishing Group, Inc.
29 East 21st Street, New York, NY 10010

Copyright © 2002 by The Rosen Publishing Group, Inc.

All rights reserved. No part of this book may be reproduced in any form without
permission in writing from the publisher, except by a reviewer.

First Edition

Book Design: Maria E. Melendez
Project Editor: Frances E. Ruffin

Photo Credits:  Cover and title page, p. 16 (the first Thanksgiving) © Burstein Collection/CORBIS; p. 4 (Pilgrims going to church, 1867), p. 12 (first Thanksgiving, 1621) © SuperStock; p. 5 (Pilgrim couple on the road to church, Plymouth colony), p. 7 ("Welcome, Englishmen" Squanto greets the Pilgrims), p. 8 (Pilgrim overlooking farm, Plymouth colony), p. 8 (the wild turkey of America, 1850s), p. 11 (Wampanoag Indians in the forest hunting for deer), p. 15 (New World crops: maize, squash, and fruit), p. 20 (Plymouth colony treaty with Massasoit), p. 21 (different colors of Indian corn (maize) and squash), p. 22 (portrait of Abraham Lincoln in 1861) © North Wind Pictures; p. 12 (seventeenth century Delft plate), p. 12 (copper alloy cauldron) © Museum of London; p. 13 (oak stools Ashby Street Ledgers Northamptonshire, seventeenth/eighteenth century, 17 inches wide), p. 14 (two basting spoons, an Elizabeth I Apostle spoon 1561, a rare William III Provincial Trefid end spoon late seventeenth century) © CHRISTIE'S IMAGES LTD; p. 19 (Pilgrim children carrying hornbooks on their way to school) © The Granger Collection.

Whitehurst, Susan.
    The first Thanksgiving / Susan Whitehurst.
        p. cm. — (The library of the Pilgrims)
        Includes index.
    ISBN 0-8239-5807-8          *30024219  12/03*
    1.  Thanksgiving Day—History—Juvenile literature.  2.  Pilgrims (New Plymouth Colony)—History—Juvenile literature.  3.  Wampanoag Indians—History—Juvenile literature.  4.  United States—Social life and customs—Juvenile literature. [1.  Thanksgiving Day—History.  2.  Pilgrims (New Plymouth Colony)—Social life and customs.]  I.  Title.
GT4975 .W47 2002
394.2649—dc21

                                                                                          00-012303

Manufactured in the United States of America

# Contents

1 The Good Harvest — 5

2 Harvest Festivals — 6

3 Company's Coming — 9

4 Welcome — 10

5 Dinner Is Served — 13

6 What They Ate — 14

7 A Three-Day Holiday — 17

8 A Time for Fun — 18

9 A Treaty — 21

10 Thanksgiving Today — 22

Glossary — 23

Index — 24

Web Sites — 24

# The Good Harvest

In the fall of 1621, the Pilgrims who lived in the Plymouth **settlement** were busy gathering a harvest. There were fields of ripe Indian corn, beans, and squash that they had planted in the summer. The Pilgrims had sailed to Plymouth almost a year before on the *Mayflower*. They had left their homes in England to find religious freedom in America. Winter set in shortly after they arrived in America. The weather was cold, much colder than what they had experienced in England. Many of the people became sick, and about half of the Pilgrims who had arrived on the *Mayflower* died before spring.

*The Pilgrims arrived in Plymouth tired from their long trip at sea, hungry because there was little food left, and sick from disease and the cold.*

*Among the families who became sick was Elizabeth Tilley's. In the autumn of 1621, Elizabeth was a 14-year-old Pilgrim girl. Elizabeth may have been one of the young Pilgrim girls and boys who went out to gather the harvest.*

5

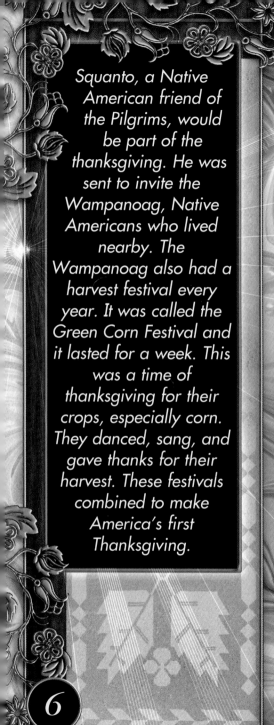

Squanto, a Native American friend of the Pilgrims, would be part of the thanksgiving. He was sent to invite the Wampanoag, Native Americans who lived nearby. The Wampanoag also had a harvest festival every year. It was called the Green Corn Festival and it lasted for a week. This was a time of thanksgiving for their crops, especially corn. They danced, sang, and gave thanks for their harvest. These festivals combined to make America's first Thanksgiving.

# Harvest Festivals

A day of thanksgiving was to be celebrated in Plymouth in the fall of 1621. William Bradford, the governor of Plymouth, announced that the Pilgrims were to have a harvest festival. This would be the first Thanksgiving in America, but the Pilgrims didn't call it Thanksgiving Day. In England, they had celebrated harvest festivals when farmers gathered their crops to store for the winter. They also observed special religious days of thanksgiving. They often spent those days praying and **fasting**. In the evenings, they had a feast.

Left: *This is an image of how a Wampanoag Indian Warrior might have looked.*
Right: *This picture shows Squanto greeting the Pilgrims.* ▶

# Company's Coming

Everyone in Plymouth prepared for the festival. Governor Bradford sent four men into the woods to hunt for wild turkeys, ducks, and geese. Only four housewives—Susanna Winslow, Elinor Billington, Elizabeth Hopkins, and Mary Brewster—had survived the winter's "great sickness" and **starvation**. Everyone helped with the cooking. Men built giant outdoor cooking fires. The boys dug for clams, trapped lobsters, and gathered nuts and berries. Girls, like Elizabeth Tilley, helped to bake round loaves of cornbread. They also helped the women turn the meat on a **spit**.

*The Pilgrims found wild turkeys in America. Turkey is a favorite food eaten during Thanksgiving.*

*The Pilgrim women and girls boiled carrots, turnips, and pumpkins. They had to be very careful to keep their long skirts away from the fires. Everyone was very busy. This meal had to feed the 52 Pilgrims and the Native Americans whom they had invited to dinner.*

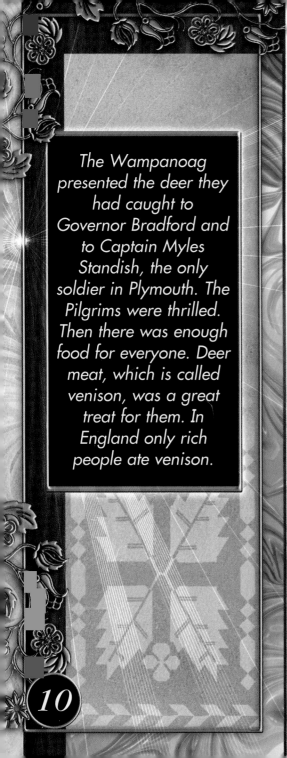

The Wampanoag presented the deer they had caught to Governor Bradford and to Captain Myles Standish, the only soldier in Plymouth. The Pilgrims were thrilled. Then there was enough food for everyone. Deer meat, which is called venison, was a great treat for them. In England only rich people ate venison.

# Welcome

When Chief Massasoit of the **Wampanoag** walked out of the forest, he was dressed for a celebration. For the special occasion, he had smoothed his hair with goose grease. He wore mooseskin moccasins, deerskin pants, and a squirrel skin coat with the fur turned to the inside for warmth. Behind him came 90 Wampanoag **braves**. The Pilgrims were shocked! If they fed everyone, all the food that they had hoped to store for the winter would be gone. Fortunately Chief Massasoit understood the problem immediately. He sent some of his men into the woods. They soon returned with five deer.

*This picture shows Wampanoag Indians in the forest hunting for deer.* ▶

# Dinner Is Served

The Pilgrims set up tables outdoors, in the only street in town. It was called The Street. Their small, one-room homes barely could hold their own families. There would be more than 140 people at dinner. The tables were **planks** of wood laid on top of barrels. The food was served on **trenchers**, which were scooped-out wooden plates. Clam shells made fine serving spoons. The Pilgrims had no forks, so eating with their fingers was not only considered good manners, it was the only way to eat. Fortunately there were lots of large, cloth napkins for holding hot meat.

◀ Top: *The Pilgrims brought this plate and pot to America.*
Below: *This painting shows the Pilgrims and Native Americans enjoying a feast.*

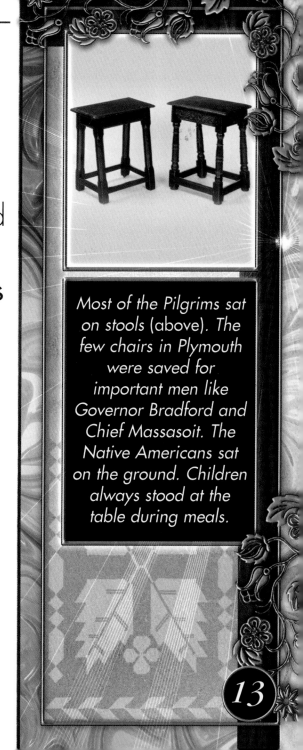

*Most of the Pilgrims sat on stools (above). The few chairs in Plymouth were saved for important men like Governor Bradford and Chief Massasoit. The Native Americans sat on the ground. Children always stood at the table during meals.*

13

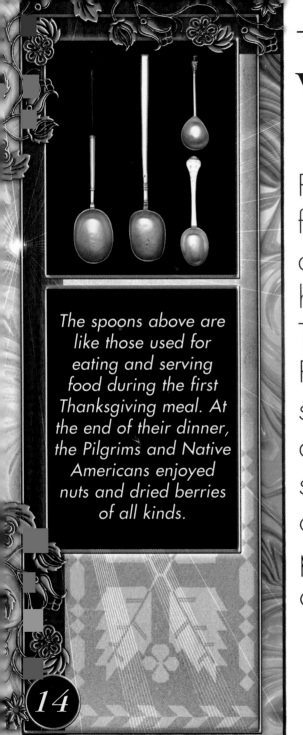

The spoons above are like those used for eating and serving food during the first Thanksgiving meal. At the end of their dinner, the Pilgrims and Native Americans enjoyed nuts and dried berries of all kinds.

# What They Ate

No one wrote down exactly what the Pilgrims and Native Americans ate during that first Thanksgiving celebration. There were many different kinds of foods available in their new home, Plymouth. What was served at that first Thanksgiving? In addition to the venison, the Pilgrims and their guests may have enjoyed seafood and fish dishes, such as codfish, eel, and clams. Peas, squash, and beans were served. Cornbread was eaten with maple syrup or honey. They made pumpkin pudding, not pie. There was no cranberry sauce. Dried cranberries were used to add flavor to foods.

*The painting shows some of the foods that the Pilgrims served and ate at their first Thanksgiving celebration.*

# A Three-Day Holiday

A Pilgrim blessing was said before dinner. They thanked God for the beautiful harvest that would feed them until next spring. They also said thanks for their homes and families, for their good friends, the Wampanoag, and for having survived the terrible winter. Then the celebration began. The Pilgrims and the Wampanoag ate and danced. They sang and played games. Then they ate some more. When evening came, the Pilgrims went home to sleep. The Wampanoag camped nearby. The next day, they got up and started all over again. The celebration went on for three days.

*The Pilgrims were thankful for many things during their first Thanksgiving celebration.*

*During the celebration, the Native Americans showed off their skills with bows and arrows. Captain Myles Standish gathered all the Pilgrim men and their musket guns and marched down The Street. It might be said that this was America's first Thanksgiving Day Parade.*

17

Footraces were run up and down The Street during the three-day holiday. Pilgrim women danced jigs to the music of the pipe and drum. Then the Wampanoag did a Native American dance. In the end, they all may have joined in a tug-of-war with both teams falling to the ground and laughing.

# A Time for Fun

The Pilgrims' lives had been so hard and busy that they had had little time for games. This first Thanksgiving was a very special time. They hadn't forgotten how to have fun, after all. The men may have played a game of Wampanoag soccer in which the goalposts were 1 mile (1.6 km) apart. The men also may have competed to test each other's strength at "pitching the bar." The man who threw the log the farthest was the winner. The children of that time played an early form of baseball called stool ball. They hit a stuffed leather ball with a bat and used stools as bases.

*After the celebration, it was back to work or school lessons for the Pilgrims.*

# A Treaty

It was a time for laughter and thanksgiving. The Pilgrims had sailed across the ocean and had found a new home. They had found good friends in the Wampanoag and especially in **Squanto**. Governor Bradford called Squanto "a special instrument sent by God." If Squanto hadn't taught the Pilgrims how to plant corn, beans, and squash, and how to hunt and fish, they might have starved to death.

To seal their friendship, the Pilgrims and the Wampanoag made a peace **treaty** during that first spring the Pilgrims were in Plymouth. This treaty lasted for more than 50 years.

◀ *Governor William Bradford and Chief Massasoit made a treaty of peace between Pilgrims and Native Americans.*

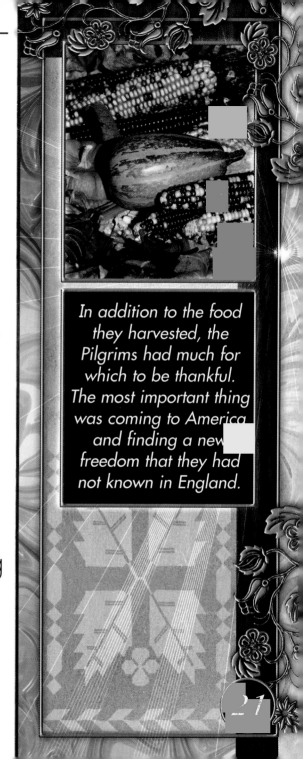

*In addition to the food they harvested, the Pilgrims had much for which to be thankful. The most important thing was coming to America and finding a new freedom that they had not known in England.*

# Thanksgiving Today

*President Abraham Lincoln made Thanksgiving a national holiday in 1863.*

America has celebrated many official days of thanksgiving. George Washington sent out a **proclamation** stating that there be a national day of thanksgiving on November 26, 1789. About 74 years later, Sarah J. Hale, a women's magazine editor, urged President Abraham Lincoln to create a thanksgiving holiday. Lincoln proclaimed that the last Thursday in November would be the national Thanksgiving Day, to be celebrated by every American. It is on this day that we continue to remember the Pilgrims and the Native Americans who started our **tradition** of Thanksgiving.

# Glossary

**braves** (BRAYVS)  Native Americans who are trained to fight.

**fasting** (FAST-ing)  Choosing to go without food.

**planks** (PLANKS)  Thick, heavy wooden boards.

**proclamation** (proh-kleh-MAY-shun)  An official announcement.

**settlement** (SEH-tul-ment)  A small village or group of houses.

**spit** (SPIT)  A metal rod that holds meat over a fire for cooking.

**Squanto** (SKWAN-to)  Squanto was the last surviving Patuxet Indian. He lived with the Pilgrims and taught them how to farm, fish, and hunt.

**starvation** (star-VAY-shun)  To suffer or die from hunger.

**tradition** (truh-DIH-shun)  A way of doing something that is passed down through the years.

**treaty** (TREE-tee)  A formal agreement, especially one between nations, signed and agreed upon by each nation.

**trenchers** (TREN-churz)  Plates of wood, or bread, that are hollowed out to hold food.

**Wampanoag** (wahm-puh-NO-ag)  A group of Native Americans who live in Massachusetts and Rhode Island.

HILLSBORO LIBRARY
HILLSBORO, OR 97123

MEMBER OF WASHINGTON COUNTY
COOPERATIVE LIBRARY SERVICES

# Index

**B**
Bradford, Governor
    William, 6, 9, 21

**E**
England, 5, 6

**F**
food, 5, 14, 21

**G**
"great sickness,"9

**H**
harvest, 5, 17
harvest festival, 6

**L**
Lincoln, President Abraham,
    22

**M**
*Mayflower*, 5
Massasoit, Chief, 10

**P**
Pilgrims, 5, 10, 13, 14,
    17, 18
Plymouth, 5, 6, 9, 14

**S**
Squanto, 21
Street, The, 13

**T**
The Street, 13
treaty, 21
trenchers, 13

**W**
Wampanoag, 10, 17, 21
Washington, George, 22

# Web Sites

To learn more about the first Thanksgiving, check out these Web sites:
www.plimoth.org
www.wilstar.com/holidays/thankstr.htm

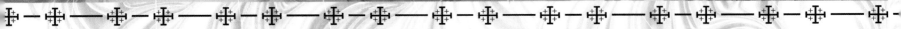